Original title:
The Frozen Silence

Author: Aron Pilviste
ISBN HARDBACK: 978-9916-79-369-5
ISBN PAPERBACK: 978-9916-79-370-1
ISBN EBOOK: 978-9916-79-371-8

A Breath of Crystal Air

In the morning light we stand,
Breath of crystal, gentle hand.
Whispers dance through frosty trees,
Nature's chill, a sweet disease.

Mountains rise with snowy crowns,
Echoes of the silent towns.
Footprints crunch on hidden trails,
Winter's song, the heart prevails.

A whisper floats on icy winds,
Time slows down, as winter binds.
In this moment, pure and rare,
We share a breath of crystal air.

Shadows of a Silent Hearth

In the glow of embers' light,
Shadows dance through the quiet night.
Whispers float like gentle ghosts,
In the warmth, we gather close.

Stories told in flickering flame,
Names and laughter, all the same.
Hearts entwined, a bond so tight,
In the shadows, love ignites.

Outside the world, a winter chill,
But here we find our hearts to fill.
In this haven, time stands still,
Together, we embrace the thrill.

Imprints in the Snow

A winter white, a pristine sheet,
Footprints mark where we once meet.
Each step taken, stories told,
Imprints left in crisp, bright cold.

Children laughing, voices bright,
Snowflakes swirling, pure delight.
In the field, our laughter flies,
Underneath the pale blue skies.

Night descends, the world aglow,
Softly covering the imprints low.
Memories linger, hearts entwine,
In the snow, your hand in mine.

The Sound of Nothingness

In the stillness, silence reigns,
A quiet world, where calm remains.
Thoughts drift softly, like the air,
Embraced by peace, a tranquil lair.

Time is fleeting, moments pause,
In the void, we find our cause.
The sound of nothing gently hums,
In the quiet, wisdom comes.

As shadows stretch and fade away,
In nothingness, we choose to stay.
Let the echoes softly cease,
Here we find our perfect peace.

Diary of a Winter Night

Cold winds whisper through the trees,
Dancing shadows in the freeze.
Stars adorn the velvet sky,
While moonlight softly bids goodbye.

Footprints lost beneath the snow,
Memories drift, all too slow.
Fires crackle, warmth bestowed,
As the winter night unfolds its ode.

Blankets wrapped around my soul,
Heartbeats echo, soft and whole.
In this stillness, dreams take flight,
The world is hushed, a pure delight.

Candles flicker, shadows play,
An honest heart finds its way.
In the glow of winter's charm,
Love and laughter keep me warm.

Tomorrow waits with gentle hope,
Through frosty winds, we learn to cope.
In every chill, there's a spark,
This winter night leaves its mark.

Glistening Silence Like Crystal

In the quiet, crystals gleam,
Frozen whispers softly stream.
Nature dresses in white lace,
Every branch, a perfect grace.

Snowflakes fall like fleeting dreams,
Blanketing all in silver beams.
Footsteps echo, soft and light,
In the stillness of the night.

Breath clouds linger in the air,
Magic woven everywhere.
With each moment, time suspends,
Glistening silence never ends.

Stars above, like diamonds glow,
Guiding pathways through the snow.
In this wonder, calm and clear,
The heart finds solace, free from fear.

Winter's canvas, pure and bright,
Painting landscapes with delight.
In this beauty, hearts unite,
Glistening silence feels so right.

The Sound of Shimmering Night

Beneath the veil of starlit skies,
Every rustle, every sigh.
Crickets serenade the moon,
Nature whispers a gentle tune.

Winds caress the quiet ground,
In this stillness, magic found.
Branches sway with softest grace,
Echos dance in this sacred space.

Shimmering shadows weave and play,
Underneath the milky way.
Time stands still, a breath we share,
In the night, we find repair.

Hearts aflame with vibrant light,
Guided by the stars so bright.
In the beauty of this glow,
The sound of night begins to flow.

Listen closely, hear the night,
In its depths, the world takes flight.
Each moment, a treasure bright,
In the sound of shimmering night.

Requiem of the Snow-Covered Meadow

A quiet field in winter's grasp,
Snowflakes fall, a gentle clasp.
Silence reigns where life once thrived,
In this hush, memories survived.

Beneath the white, dreams linger still,
Secrets hidden, time to fill.
Every drift a tale untold,
In this meadow, moments cold.

The whispering breeze recalls the past,
Echoes fading, shadows cast.
Time moves slow, yet quick it flies,
In its essence, love complies.

Branches bow, adorned with grace,
Nature’s beauty, soft embrace.
In this requiem, hearts can mend,
Whispers of winter never end.

So let us walk through fields of white,
Finding peace in the soft light.
In the quiet, we shall find,
Hope and solace intertwined.

A Tryst with Winter's Vow

In twilight's clutch, a canvas white,
Frosted whispers weave through the night.
Silent shadows dance, hearts entwined,
In the cloak of snow, love defined.

Breezes chill, yet warmth we cling,
Beneath the stars, our spirits sing.
Fires blaze in hushed repose,
As winter's breath softly blows.

We carve our dreams in frozen streams,
In breathless air, we sketch our schemes.
Every flake tells tales anew,
Of the vows we softly woo.

Candles flicker in the pallor pale,
Our laughter, like a gentle gale.
The world outside fades to a hush,
In winter's kiss, we find our rush.

Morning breaks with gleaming frost,
But in this moment, no love is lost.
For in the cold, warmth we find,
A tryst, forever, intertwined.

Restoration of the Frigid Soul

Amidst the chill, a quiet plea,
For warmth to rise from memory.
Like lonesome trees in crystal glaze,
I search for light in winter's maze.

A gentle breeze whispers my name,
In this harsh world, I play the game.
Each snowflake carries dreams of old,
Restoring fragments, brave and bold.

Frozen waters crack and churn,
Beneath the ice, the embers burn.
With every heartbeat, I shall mend,
The frigid soul that longs to blend.

Through frozen paths, I tread with grace,
Finding solace in this space.
A beacon in the dark night spreads,
An inner warmth, as hope embeds.

Though winter's grasp may feel profound,
In quietude, my strength is found.
For as the snow begins to melt,
A brighter dawn shall soon be felt.

Glacial Lullabies of the Night

Underneath the crescent moon,
The night hums a glacial tune.
Softly wrapped in silver rays,
We drift through winter’s mystic maze.

Stars like icicles drip and sway,
In the hush, dreams lead the way.
Beneath the quilt of twinkling light,
We breathe in deep the frosty night.

Whispers swirl as shadows roam,
In this chill, we find our home.
Each breath a frosted sigh released,
As winter’s lullabies increase.

Echoes of a warmth once known,
In the frost, our love has grown.
With every note twinkling bright,
We sing along to the starry night.

Crystals form where memories linger,
As dreams weave patterns through our fingers.
In the depths of winter’s song,
We find the place where we belong.

Veiled Secrets of Winter's Hold

Whispers cling to the frosty air,
Silver trees stand, an ancient glare.
In the hush of a chilling night,
Secrets bound in soft moonlight.

Frosted breath, a fleeting sigh,
Underneath the velvet sky.
Time is still, as shadows creep,
Winter's promise, a dream to keep.

Beneath the snow, the world concealed,
Nature's heart, gently healed.
Branches bow with laden weight,
Yearning softly, love and fate.

Echoed steps on crisp white ground,
Every sound feels unbound.
Frozen paths that twist and turn,
In the quiet, passions burn.

Veiled whispers in the cold,
Every tale yet untold.
Layers thick with silent wishes,
Winter's charm, lost in kisses.

Shadows of Silence Across Snow

In shadows deep, where whispers lie,
Silence reigns under the sky.
Snowflakes dance with tender grace,
In their descent, a soft embrace.

Footprints linger, moments passed,
Echos of the heart, unsurpassed.
Wrapped in white, the world stands still,
Peaceful sighs, the heart they fill.

Glistening crystals catch the light,
Night unfolds, embracing night.
Hushed secrets in the frost,
In winter's grace, we find our lost.

As shadows stretch, a sigh of peace,
Worries fade, and sorrows cease.
In this realm of white and grey,
Tomorrow waits, a hopeful day.

Beneath the snow, the dreams reside,
Waiting gently, hearts confide.
In winter's hold, we're not alone,
In every flake, a story's grown.

Icebound Melancholy

Trapped in silence, hearts collide,
An icy grip we cannot hide.
Longing stirs within the freeze,
Where time lingers, memories tease.

Beneath the frost, a river flows,
Hidden dreams the cold wind knows.
Shadows woven with gentle sighs,
Underneath these heavy skies.

Every flake a fallen tear,
From distant hopes, both bright and sheer.
Winds of change softly swirl,
While the icy grip makes hearts twirl.

Melancholy’s quiet song,
In the night, it won’t be long.
Embers wait for spring's embrace,
In the chill, we find our place.

Layers thick, yet hearts remain,
In this longing, sweet as pain.
All the love that winter brings,
Wrapped in silence, hope still sings.

The Quiet Shiver of Dreams

In the twilight, shadows play,
Dreams reside in soft array.
Whispers glide on wintry breath,
In this stillness, life feels death.

Frozen moments, captured grace,
Within the cold, a warm embrace.
Hopes that shimmer in the dark,
Light the path, a hopeful spark.

Under starlight, dreams unfold,
Cloaked in quiet, tales retold.
Silent wishes, gently spun,
In the hush of night, we run.

Each heartbeat echoes in the still,
Painting landscapes, bending will.
A shiver wraps around the heart,
In the dreamscape, we depart.

When morning breaks, the silence wanes,
In that light, a spark remains.
Though night may hold its quiet schemes,
The dawn will rise, fulfilling dreams.

Half-Remembered Stories in the Frost

Whispers of tales in the winter air,
Frosted edges where memories cling.
Steps in the snow lead us there,
To places where dreams take wing.

Pale shadows dance in the morning light,
Echoes of laughter, a fleeting trace.
Lost in the quiet, the world feels right,
As shards of the past interlace.

Glimmers of warmth in the icy breath,
Bring stories hidden beneath the chill.
Each breath a moment, a dance with death,
Carving our paths with steadfast will.

Though time may blur the lines we draw,
In frost-kissed nights, we find our way.
Heartbeats align with nature's law,
We cherish the night, embrace the day.

So let each step be a tale retold,
In whispers of frost, our souls set free.
Together we weave the warmth from cold,
In half-remembered stories, you and me.

Fragments of Sound Within Ice

A creaking hush fills the frosty air,
Where silence holds the world in thrall.
Each snap of frost, a gentle prayer,
In nature's grasp, we hear it all.

Crystalline whispers, a melody near,
Tangled notes in the glacier's song.
Echoes of life rise crystalline clear,
Lost in the beauty that feels so strong.

Rustling leaves in the frozen hush,
Dancing gently on the frozen ground.
Moments of magic in life's soft rush,
Fragments of sound where peace is found.

Underneath blankets of swirling white,
The heartbeats echo, a soft embrace.
Each note of winter, a silent light,
Carving memories in time and space.

So listen well to the ice's song,
Feel the pulse of the world's embrace.
In fragments of sound, we all belong,
In icy realms we find our place.

Nature’s Quiet Cloak

The world draped softly in silver hue,
Wrapped in whispers, a gentle shroud.
Nature's quiet cloak, the old and new,
Stillness descending; it speaks aloud.

Beneath the frost, the earth holds dreams,
Hidden treasures in slumber deep.
Where sunlight glistens, and moonlight gleams,
In nature's embrace, we safely sleep.

The trees stand tall, their branches bare,
Adorned with crystals, they gleam and sway.
In the softest breath, there's magic there,
Nature holds secrets in shadowy play.

Through frozen fields, the silence roams,
Kissed by a wind that whispers low.
With each soft step, we find our homes,
In the quiet cloak, our spirits grow.

So let us wander where the stillness calls,
In nature's embrace, our worries cease.
For in her quiet, the heart enthralls,
Wrapped in the cloak of timeless peace.

Poise Beneath the Glimmer

Stars twinkle softly in a velvet sky,
Each one a beacon, a tale to share.
In quiet corners where dreams lie,
We hold our hopes with tender care.

Beneath the glimmer, the world awakes,
Whispers of night in a cosmic dance.
The pulse of the universe gently shakes,
Offering us a fleeting chance.

With every breath, we draw in light,
Embracing the darkness, we learn to soar.
In still moments, our hearts take flight,
Finding balance in the evermore.

As shadows linger and time unfolds,
We stand in grace, a steady flame.
Through silver mist and stories told,
With poise beneath the glimmer, we claim.

So let the stars be our guiding map,
On paths we wander, both near and far.
In the quiet night, there's no mishap,
For poise beneath the glimmer is who we are.

Frozen Harmonies Lost in Time

In the stillness, echoes dwell,
Notes of ages, a silent spell.
Snowflakes dance on a winter's breath,
Whispers soft, the song of death.

Beneath the ice, a tale unfolds,
Of ancient dreams, in silence told.
Frozen winds, they weave and twine,
Bound within this world divine.

Crystals shimmer, reflecting light,
Mysteries held within the night.
Time stands still, yet moves so fast,
Moments captured, shadows cast.

Each note a memory, soft and clear,
Resonating through frozen sphere.
Harmony lost but never gone,
In the heart of winter's song.

So linger here, in the cold embrace,
Find your solace, your sacred space.
Among the echoes, find your rhyme,
In frozen harmonies lost in time.

Whispers from the Glacier's Heart

Deep within the glacier's core,
Whispers speak of tales of yore.
Layers thick with memory steep,
Secrets guarded, watch them keep.

Cracks and crevices tell their tale,
Of nature's strength, a silent gale.
Icebound stories start to flow,
From ancient depths where cold winds blow.

Each fracture sings a different tune,
A lullaby beneath the moon.
Echoes ripple through the frozen blue,
Softly calling, beckoning you.

In the realm where silence reigns,
Whispers linger in frozen chains.
Listen closely to the part,
Of subtle secrets from the heart.

So wander deep through icy halls,
Where the glacier's whisper calls.
Embrace the chill, let it start,
To weave its magic in your heart.

The Unseen Serenade of Quiet

In the silence of the night,
A serenade, pure delight.
Notes unheard, yet deeply felt,
In every heart, emotions melt.

Softly drifts the winter's breeze,
Carrying secrets among the trees.
Harmony hides in stillness high,
Waiting patiently to reveal why.

Stars hanging low, a gentle glow,
Illuminating paths we know.
In unseen spaces, music breathes,
Lifting spirits like autumn leaves.

Listen closely, close your eyes,
To the whispers beneath the skies.
A symphony of calm and peace,
In the unseen, our thoughts release.

So cherish moments, quiet, deep,
Where hidden melodies softly creep.
For in the stillness, dreams lie unspun,
A serenade shared by everyone.

Layers of Ice and Their Secrets

Beneath the surface, stories sleep,
In layers deep, the secrets keep.
Frozen tales of joy and woe,
Within the ice, a world we sow.

Each layer formed by time's embrace,
Capturing moments in their place.
Whispers locked in crystal threads,
Tales of laughter, tears, and dread.

In the stillness, voices blend,
A chorus of the past to mend.
Unraveling truths, we can see,
The beauty of our history.

Crystalline echoes, clear and bright,
Shooting stars in the velvet night.
Layer by layer, they unfold,
The stories waiting to be told.

So venture forth, let curiosity steer,
Into the depths where memories peer.
Through layers of ice, let us traverse,
To uncover the universe's verse.

Breathless Landscapes

Waves of green roll under skies,
Mountains stretch with open eyes.
Fields of gold in the setting sun,
Whispers of nature, never done.

Rivers dance through valleys wide,
Carrying dreams on the swift tide.
Branches sway with the gentle breeze,
Nature's symphony brings sweet ease.

Echoes linger in the air,
Marking moments, rich and rare.
Each step taken on this ground,
In every heartbeat, beauty found.

Stars alight in the cosmic sea,
Guiding souls who long to be.
Breathless tales in every view,
Nature's canvas, forever new.

In rugged cliffs and open plains,
Life thrives within its joyful chains.
Crafted by hands unseen, divine,
Breathless landscapes, yours and mine.

Solitude Wrapped in White

Snowflakes fall like silent sighs,
Blanketing earth, cloaking ties.
Each breath taken, crisp and clear,
In this stillness, all is near.

Bare trees stand in quiet grace,
Nature's canvas, a serene space.
Footprints mark the path we tread,
In solitude, sweet thoughts are spread.

Whispers dance on winter's breath,
Frosty air holds thoughts of death.
Yet in this chill, warmth can bloom,
Amidst the frost, dreams find room.

Moonlight spills on the frozen ground,
Peace surrounds, a sacred sound.
Wrapped in white, shadows blend,
Solitude, my quiet friend.

Each moment lingers, soft embrace,
In this silence, I find my place.
With every snowstorm that sways,
Solitude wrapped in winter's gaze.

Time Encased in Frost

Icicles hang from eaves like tears,
Each one traps the passing years.
Moments frozen, whispers caught,
In the stillness, time is sought.

A clock ticks slow in the hush,
Quiet nights blend into a rush.
Frosty mornings greet the dawn,
When warmth returns, the chill is gone.

Windows fogged with the breath of age,
Silence wrapped in a timeless cage.
Memories linger, drifting slow,
In frozen frames, they come and go.

Time, a thread of crystal spun,
In the cold light of the sun.
Each hour marked by snow's soft kiss,
Encased in frost, we find our bliss.

As seasons change, we learn to hold,
The fleeting moments, young and old.
Time encased, yet always flows,
In winter's grasp, the heart still knows.

Lullabies of the Frozen World

Night descends, the stars ignite,
Whispers of the silent night.
Crystals shimmer in moon’s glow,
Lullabies of the frost below.

Snow blankets all in softest hush,
An enchanted world in twilight’s blush.
Every heartbeat, soft and low,
Cradled in winter's tender flow.

Winds carry songs from distant lands,
With gentle grace, the minute stands.
Each breath a note in nature's choir,
Lullabies woven of dreams and fire.

Owls call out in rhythmic tones,
Echoes dance in frozen zones.
Wrapped in layers, warm and tight,
The frozen world sings through the night.

In this realm of white and gold,
Every story quietly told.
Lullabies of peace and grace,
In the frost, we find our place.

Serenity Suspended in Time

In quiet woods where shadows play,
The sunlight weaves a golden ray.
Leaves dance softly in the breeze,
Whispered secrets among the trees.

A gentle stream flows by with grace,
Reflecting nature's calm embrace.
Moments linger, soft and bright,
As day transforms to velvet night.

Stars awaken, one by one,
Painting dreams 'til night is done.
In this stillness, hearts align,
Finding peace in moments divine.

Time stands still, we breathe anew,
In every shade, in every hue.
Here in silence, we ignite,
Love's eternal, soft delight.

In this realm where spirits soar,
Boundless dreams forever more.
Serenity, a fleeting time,
In nature's arms, we find our rhyme.

When Nature Holds Its Breath

Fog blankets the world in gray,
Silence whispers, nature's sway.
Branches bend with unspoken words,
As life pauses, still like birds.

The air is thick with thought and awe,
Every creature, still, we draw.
In this moment, echoes hide,
Time suspended, heart open wide.

Drop of dew on leaf so frail,
Nature's secret, quiet tale.
Hushed the world, in waiting state,
Every heartbeat, a gentle fate.

Then a rustle, life awakes,
Breath of wind through silence breaks.
Nature stirs, a vibrant sound,
In this dance, we are all found.

When the frost begins to melt,
It's in that warmth, true life is felt.
Nature smiles, its breath renewed,
In every shade, in every mood.

Frostbitten Memories

In winter's grasp, where cold winds blow,
Frozen echoes of long ago.
Whispers trapped in icy lace,
Youthful laughter, fleeting grace.

Footprints in snow, a tale untold,
Crystals shimmer, hearts turn bold.
Each flake falls like a forgotten prayer,
As memories hang in the frigid air.

A warm hearth beckons, light aglow,
Holding stories of long ago.
Hot cocoa warms cold, tired hands,
While outside, winter's magic stands.

Nostalgia dances in frosty light,
Returning joy in winter's night.
In whispered tales of all that’s lost,
Warmth and love outweigh the frost.

Frostbitten dreams may fade away,
Still, time pauses for hearts that stay.
Through bitter chill, hope softly sings,
In every ending, new life springs.

Echoes of a Hidden Realm

Beneath the surface, secrets lurk,
In shadows deep where dreamers work.
Whispers float on moonlit streams,
Echoing softly, lost in dreams.

The forest holds its breath in awe,
Magic breathes in every flaw.
Little critters dance through night,
In their world, everything's right.

Stars ignite the velvet skies,
Igniting wonder in our eyes.
Hidden realms, a call to roam,
Every heartbeat leads us home.

Ancient trees stand tall and wise,
Guarding tales beneath the skies.
Nature's voice, a gentle nudge,
In every path, a sacred grudge.

With each step on this earthen maze,
We uncover the hidden ways.
Echoes linger, soft and bright,
Guiding souls through velvet night.

Frozen Murmurs

Whispers of winter chill,
Echoes in the silent night,
Softly through the frosted air,
Time lingers, frozen tight.

Crystal branches arching high,
Sparkle under pale moon's gleam,
Nature sleeps beneath the sky,
Wrapped within a silver dream.

Footprints trace the snowy ground,
Secrets hidden, softly spoken,
In this hush, a world is found,
Fragile bonds, unbroken.

Every flake, a tale to tell,
Of seasons past, of life anew,
In the stillness, all is well,
A tapestry of white and blue.

Frozen murmurs, soft and low,
Crystals glisten, hearts will sway,
In this moment's gentle flow,
Winter's breath will fade away.

A Veil of Ice and Quiet

A curtain hangs of frosted lace,
Soft whispers weave amidst the trees,
In the shade, still dreams embrace,
As snowflakes twirl upon the breeze.

Silence wraps the world in white,
Each branch dons a sparkling crown,
Guided by the pale moonlight,
Nature wears her crystal gown.

Footsteps muffled in the glade,
Echoes of the day long gone,
In the woodland, plans are laid,
Underneath the frosty dawn.

A hush envelopes all around,
Time stands still, both vast and small,
In this peace, a truth is found,
Where the heart can hear the call.

A veil of ice, a world transformed,
In the quiet, life takes flight,
Amidst the frozen, warmth is formed,
In this beauty, pure delight.

Shadows Wrapped in Frost

Dusk descends, the day does fade,
Shadows stretch and intertwine,
Frosty whispers softly played,
Nature shimmers, pure design.

Soft clouds drift on silver streams,
Casting secrets of the night,
In the hush, enchantment gleams,
Underneath the starlit light.

Every breath a vapor's dance,
In the cool, a moment still,
Frozen magic, a trance,
Filling hearts with winter's thrill.

Branches bow beneath the weight,
Of icy jewels, gleaming bright,
In this world of crystalline fate,
Every shadow takes to flight.

Shadows wrapped in frost entwine,
A tapestry of night and day,
Within silence, stars align,
In this frozen ballet.

The Serenity of Still Air

Calm descends, a gentle pause,
In the stillness, peace resides,
Winter's breath without a cause,
Magnolia dreams where hope abides.

Branches stand, a silent vow,
Waiting for the spring's embrace,
Time in quiet moments slow,
In the air, a crisp, sweet grace.

Pale light bathes the frozen ground,
Soft shadows dance in twilight's glow,
Nature holds its breath, profound,
In this embrace, the world will grow.

A moment's peace is all we seek,
Amid the chill that paints the skies,
In still air, the heart does speak,
Through frost, a warmth never dies.

The serenity of still air,
Whispers secrets, time will tell,
In the quiet, love lays bare,
In the frost, all is well.

Veil of Frosted Dreams

In the quiet of the night,
Whispers drift like snowflakes,
Softly cloaked in silver light,
Time itself gently breaks.

Beneath a shroud of icy breath,
Secrets sleep in shadows deep,
Echoes linger, dance with death,
In the stillness, silence weep.

A tapestry of frozen grace,
Each moment caught, a fleeting gleam,
Nature paints a wondrous space,
A world wrapped in a dream.

Glistening on the windowpane,
Memories twirl in swirling mist,
A realm where joy meets quiet pain,
In dreams that we have kissed.

Awake at dawn, the frost will fade,
Yet beauty lingers on the breeze,
In every path that we have laid,
A map of soft unease.

Chilling Serenity on the Wind

A breath of cold wraps round my face,
The world, a canvas painted white,
In the hush, I find my space,
Where heart and soul take flight.

Branches sway with gentle grace,
Carrying whispers from the skies,
Nature's hymn, a soft embrace,
In the stillness, beauty lies.

Each gust a fleeting, soft caress,
Calling forth the distant stars,
In the silence, I confess,
My dreams take shape, free from scars.

Amidst the chill, I find my peace,
As snowflakes twirl and dance around,
With every sigh, my worries cease,
In this calm, my heart is found.

Chilling winds that gently sing,
A lullaby beneath the trees,
In their song, new hopes take wing,
As I drift on the breeze.

Lament of the Hushed Woods

Through the forest, shadows creep,
Ancient trees stand tall and grim,
In their silence, secrets keep,
Echoing the song of whim.

Lost are voices once so clear,
The laughter of the days gone by,
In the stillness, I draw near,
A tear falls for the days that fly.

Branches weep with heavy mist,
Footfalls muffled, soft and slow,
Nature’s heart begins to twist,
In this vibrant, muted glow.

Every sigh a muted call,
To the spirits weaving through,
In the quiet, I feel small,
Yet, united with the view.

With each rustle, memories sigh,
Guardians of the tales untold,
In the woods where echoes lie,
Time’s embrace, both warm and cold.

Soft Footfalls on White

Step by step, the world transforms,
A blanket soft, a silent sheet,
In the hush, the heart conforms,
To nature's gentle, rhythmic beat.

Underneath the arching boughs,
Footprints lightly trace their path,
While the earth, in quiet bows,
Welcomes winter’s tender wrath.

Frosted branches glimmer bright,
Each sparkle sings a story old,
Of whispered dreams in soft twilight,
Where warmth is hidden, yet bold.

Each movement kissed with silver dew,
Disturbing peace in fields of white,
In this dance, my spirit flew,
A fleeting moment, pure delight.

And when the day fades into night,
The stars emerge with quiet grace,
In soft footfalls on snow’s white,
I find my place, my sacred space.

Hibernation of Sound

Whispers fade in the chill of night,
Silence blankets the world in white.
Echoes of laughter lost from the air,
Time stands still in the frozen glare.

The trees hold secrets beneath their frost,
Memories linger in what was lost.
Moonlight dances on crystals bright,
In the stillness, our dreams take flight.

Footsteps muffled on a tapestry pure,
Softly trailing where hearts endure.
Wrapped in warmth, we seek the profound,
As nature rests in hibernation's sound.

A slumber deep where echoes cease,
In the arms of winter, find your peace.
Stillness weaves through each frozen breath,
A soft embrace in the face of death.

Yet dreams awaken as spring draws near,
Revivals bloom with the warmth of cheer.
In the quiet realms of the silent ground,
Life will stir from hibernation's sound.

Snowbound Reverie

Drifting flakes in a twilight glow,
Painting landscapes where soft winds blow.
Fields of white stretch far and wide,
In the stillness, let our wishes glide.

Wrapped in warmth, we watch the scene,
A snowbound canvas, so fresh and clean.
Thoughts arise like the clouds above,
In this wonder, we find our love.

Frosted branches, an artist’s hand,
Crafting beauty on winter’s strand.
Nightingale silence, the world asleep,
Secrets buried in layers deep.

Footprints wander on a path unknown,
Where memories gather, seeds are sown.
The heart remembers the tales of old,
In the snowbound reverie, dreams unfold.

Life pauses soft beneath the stars,
Hiding wonder in the night’s memoirs.
A blanket woven from dreams and sighs,
In the snowbound world, our spirit flies.

Enigma of the Cold Void

Stars whisper softly in the cold abyss,
Each flicker a promise, a starry kiss.
Galaxies spin in a cosmic dance,
In the cold void, we seek our chance.

Shadows of time stretch far and deep,
Waves of silence where stardust sleeps.
Mysteries linger in the dark expanse,
In the void's embrace, our fears advance.

Nebulas cradle the dreams we weave,
Unraveled truths are hard to believe.
The cosmos echo with secrets untold,
In the enigma, our stories unfold.

Rivers of light through the emptiness wade,
Tracing the paths where destinies fade.
In the cold void, we search for grace,
Through endless night, we find our place.

Yet hope glimmers in the darkest night,
A beacon guiding our hearts toward light.
In the vast unknown where shadows suit,
The enigma whispers, we are astute.

Quietude in the Arctic Dawn

Morning breaks with a gentle sigh,
A palette of colors against the sky.
Whispers of sunlight kiss the frost,
In the arctic stillness, no moment lost.

Snowflakes shimmer, a grand display,
Nature’s canvas in soft array.
The world awakens from dark’s embrace,
In quietude, we find our place.

Icebergs shimmer like diamonds rare,
Carving patterns in the crisp, cold air.
A breath of fresh, untainted bliss,
In the dawn’s embrace, we find our kiss.

Footsteps crunch on the frozen ground,
Every sound an echo profound.
In the beauty of the morning light,
The arctic whispers soft and bright.

As day unfolds with grace anew,
Our hearts align with the world’s view.
In quietude, we breathe and reflect,
In the arctic dawn, we find connect.

Secrets Entrapped in Hoarfrost

Whispers dance in the cold air,
Memories shrouded in white mist,
Frozen tales we dare not share,
Bound by time, they still persist.

Around the trees, they cling tight,
Crystals glisten, secrets old,
Nature’s breath in silver light,
Stories of warmth, silently told.

Deep in shadows, truths conspire,
Frosty layers conceal the past,
Each crystal holds a heart's desire,
A fleeting breath, a life amassed.

In the silence, hear them sigh,
Echoes trapped in nature's grip,
Frosted dreams that flutter by,
On winter's chill, we take a trip.

With every step upon the ground,
Footprints vanish, lost to time,
In the stillness, they are found,
Secrets woven, frost sublime.

Breaths of Crystal Echoes

Beneath the stars, the night unfolds,
Crystals form where warmth departs,
Whispers trail in the icy holds,
Echoes wrapped in frozen arts.

Every breath a fragile sound,
Glimmers sparkling with each word,
In this world, where dreams are found,
Voices fade, yet still are heard.

Olden tales in whispers weave,
Framed in frost, they dance and play,
Every sigh a night reprieve,
In the hush, they drift away.

Snowflakes fall, each unique fall,
Patterns etched in quiet grace,
Breath of winter, softest call,
The crystal echoes leave their trace.

Listen close to the tales they share,
In the chill where souls reside,
Breaths of magic linger there,
In crystal echoes, hearts collide.

Distant Footsteps in a Frozen World

In the expanse of winter's gaze,
Footsteps echo soft and light,
Hidden paths in frozen haze,
Lost in shadows of the night.

The ground beneath, a canvas white,
Every step a fleeting mark,
Tracing paths from day to night,
In the tussle between bright and dark.

Across the fields where silence reigns,
Whispers carried on the breeze,
Frosty air, like gentle chains,
Holding moments, memories tease.

Distant echoes of the past,
Merely shadows in the snow,
Footprints fade, but love can last,
In the heart, the warmth will grow.

In this frozen, quiet sphere,
Step by step, we leave our sign,
Though the world may disappear,
In our hearts, the light will shine.

The Stillness of Winter's Embrace

Veils of white blanket the earth,
Winter whispers, soft and near,
Stillness wrapped around its worth,
In this calm, we hold our fear.

Frozen branches stretch and bend,
Crystals weave through each and all,
In the quiet, hearts can mend,
As the softest snowflakes fall.

Time seems paused in the cool air,
Moments freeze in nature's grasp,
In the silence, hope lays bare,
A gentle touch, a comforting clasp.

Underneath the starlit sky,
Dreams take flight on winds so bright,
Moments pass, but they don't die,
In winter's hold, we find our light.

In this stillness, fears release,
As we draw from nature's grace,
Winter's breath brings us to peace,
In embrace, we find our place.

Echoing Heartbeats in the Chill

In the silence of the night,
Whispers dance like fireflies,
Hearts beat in the shadows,
Carrying secrets and sighs.

Moonlight kisses the frost,
Each breath a wisp of mist,
A love that won't be lost,
In the chill, we exist.

Branches creak under weight,
Nature's lullaby sings low,
Time moves slowly, it's fate,
In the stillness, we grow.

Footsteps crunch on the ground,
Echoes of dreams untold,
In this beauty, we're bound,
Through the winter, we hold.

Embers fade, yet we glow,
Hearts beating soft and true,
In the chill, we both know,
Eternity waits for us two.

A Symphony of Permafrost

In the depths of icy blue,
A melody gently plays,
Frosted notes that weave anew,
In this silence, the heart sways.

Sharp winds cut like a knife,
Yet harmonies arise,
Nature sings of winter life,
Underneath a starlit guise.

Each crystal tells a tale,
Of moments lost in time,
In this frozen, hushed veil,
We find rhythm in the rhyme.

Beneath layers of white,
Dreams linger in the cold,
A symphony ignites,
With stories yet to be told.

As dawn paints skies with fire,
The song will never cease,
In this realm of desire,
We find solace and peace.

Fables of Frozen Landscapes

Tales unravel in the snow,
Whispers echo through the trees,
Where the northern lights glow,
And the world bends at its knees.

Mountains stand like old guards,
Watching seasons come and go,
In their silence, they regard,
The fables only they know.

Frozen rivers weave through time,
Stories etched in each bend,
Nature’s canvas, pure and sublime,
Inviting hearts to transcend.

In the embrace of the cold,
Legends rise with the sun,
Through the silence, they unfold,
Each journey just begun.

Voices carried on the breeze,
Recounting tales of the brave,
In these frosty, ancient seas,
We find the warmth we crave.

Cryogenics of the Soul

Deep within this frozen realm,
Souls awaken from their sleep,
In the stillness, they overwhelm,
Memories buried, secrets keep.

Icicles reach towards the sky,
Like fingers grasping for the past,
In each breath, a silent cry,
Wishes whispered, shadows cast.

Time unfurls in frozen waves,
Echoes bite like winter's chill,
Within the heart, the spirit braves,
Finding strength, defying will.

Crystals shimmer in moonlight,
Each glimmer, a glimpse of the whole,
Hope ignites in the night,
Healing is the cryogenic role.

In the depths, we break our chains,
Emerging from the icy hole,
Freedom dances in our veins,
An anthem for the soul.

Hushed Whispers in the Snow

Gentle flakes begin to fall,
Softly covering all in white.
Nature holds her breath in awe,
As silence wraps the world so tight.

Footprints vanish without a trace,
Whispers linger, secrets shared.
Underneath the icy grace,
Winter’s magic, pure and bare.

Trees stand tall, their branches bow,
Crystals glisten under the sun.
In this peace, we feel the now,
A moment where all time is spun.

Birds are hushed, their songs postponed,
A canvas blank, the world anew.
In this quiet, we feel honed,
Hushed whispers in the snow, it's true.

Through the night, the stars will glow,
Guiding dreams in frosty air.
Wrapped in warmth, let soft winds blow,
In our hearts, we hold this care.

The Calm Before the Blizzard

Clouds gather, heavy and gray,
A stillness settles, thick and deep.
Nature seems to pause and sway,
In this moment, secrets keep.

Trees stand quiet, waiting the storm,
Wind whispers tales of what shall be.
A calm few feel, a rare form,
Before wild winds bring liberty.

The world holds breath, a sacred lore,
Time stretches thin, yet feels so grand.
In this hush, we crave for more,
A touch from nature's gentle hand.

Snowflakes linger in the air,
Suspended dreams, a space divine.
Moments blend in nature's care,
We grasp this peace, this silent sign.

Then silence brews a rumbling thrill,
The blizzard craves to set things free.
A world transformed by winter's will,
Awaits beyond what we can see.

Captured in Ice

Frozen moments hang in time,
A crystal world, reflections bright.
Nature’s art, a silent rhyme,
Captured beauty, pure delight.

Icicles drape from branches bare,
Glistening like a dream undone.
Each shard tells tales of winter's care,
Beneath the warmth of fading sun.

A lake holds secrets, sealed so tight,
Its surface quiet, sleek, and smooth.
Dancing lightly in fading light,
The icy grip, its gentle soothe.

Winds howl softly through the trees,
Nature breathes a frosty sigh.
In this world, with such unease,
We find ourselves, just you and I.

Memories etched in frozen seams,
Eternally held in nature's heart.
In the quiet, we weave our dreams,
Together, never to be apart.

Reflections of a Shimmering Silence

Moonlight dances on the snow,
Each flake, a whisper in the night.
Quiet glimmers, soft and slow,
Reflecting magic, pure and bright.

Past the trees, a hush prevails,
Stars invite the cold to play.
Underneath this serene veil,
Shimmering silence leads the way.

Frosted breath, a gentle sigh,
Nature rests, wrapped in a dream.
In the stillness, we wonder why,
Life moves like a flowing stream.

Moments linger like the dawn,
Soft hues paint the sky anew.
In this frame, we find the fawn,
In silence, we hear nature's cue.

As dawn breaks, the world will wake,
Echoes from the night retreat.
In the calm, new paths we take,
In shimmering silence, hearts will meet.

Muted Crystals in Time

Crystals glimmer in soft light,
Frozen moments take their flight.
Time stands still, a gentle pause,
In the silence, nature’s laws.

Shadows dance on winter's breath,
Whispers echo, life and death.
Each shard holds a secret dream,
In stillness, we feel the gleam.

Frozen echoes in the air,
Every crystal, light to share.
They shimmer under pale moon's glow,
A tranquil world where we can go.

In the quiet, stories bloom,
Every crystal erases gloom.
Silent wonders softly chime,
In the realm of muted time.

Embrace the beauty, let it be,
Crystals whisper, wild and free.
Here in the stillness, we reside,
Finding peace where dreams abide.

Subdued Whispers of the Frost

Frosty breath upon the glass,
Nature’s art, a fleeting class.
Subtle whispers, crisp and clear,
In the silence, all we hear.

Veils of white on sleeping ground,
Echoes soft, a muted sound.
Fingers trace the icy lace,
In this hush, we find our place.

Morning breaks, a gentle light,
Transforming frost to pure delight.
Shadows linger, fading fast,
Time entwined in nature’s cast.

Whispers linger in the trees,
Swaying softly with the breeze.
Every flake a story told,
In the quiet, hearts unfold.

Embrace the calm, let it last,
In the frosted spell, we're cast.
Moments freeze in fleeting thought,
Subdued whispers, beauty caught.

Tranquil Desolation

In the stillness, shadows cast,
Whispers of the void hold fast.
Amidst the barren, beauty lies,
Silent echoes, distant sighs.

Lonely trees, a stark refrain,
Nature's heart knows loss and gain.
In desolation, dreams take flight,
Searching for the lost daylight.

Layers deep of silent snow,
Each breath taken, soft and slow.
Footprints parked on paths unknown,
In this realm, we feel alone.

Yet in quiet, strength we find,
Resilience blooms, unconfined.
Through the emptiness appears,
Hope that conquers all our fears.

Desolation, calm yet bright,
Holding secrets, pure delight.
In tranquil depths, we learn to see,
The soul's reflection, wild and free.

Where Silence Meets the Snowflakes

Snowflakes dance in swirling flight,
Softly falling, pure and white.
Where silence reigns, they land with grace,
Painting nature’s gentle face.

In the stillness, hearts collide,
Finding warmth where dreams abide.
Each flake tells a tale untold,
In the hush, we watch unfold.

Crystal patterns weave the air,
Fleeting beauty, moments rare.
With every breath, the quiet flows,
In the snow, a magic grows.

Gathered whispers touch the ground,
Layers deep, a magic found.
Here, where silence meets the snow,
A tranquil space where spirits glow.

The world transforms beneath the white,
In the quiet, pure delight.
Where silence wraps the winter's night,
We find solace, soft and bright.

Winter's Solitude

In the hush of falling snow,
Bare branches reach for sky,
Moon's glow a silver halo,
Whispers of the night sigh.

Footprints fade in gleaming white,
Silence wraps the earth tight,
Stars flicker, cold and bright,
Nature's breath, soft and light.

Frosted winds weave through trees,
Carrying tales of the cold,
A world steeped in quiet ease,
In chill, the heart turns bold.

The brook lies still, its voice hushed,
Ice cloaks the water's song,
In the stillness, dreams are crushed,
Time lingers, yet feels long.

Within this frozen embrace,
Moments pulse like a drum,
Winter's love, a gentle grace,
In solitude, we become.

The Weight of Frigid Air

Beneath a canopy of gray,
Frozen breath fills the space,
Each heartbeat slows to play,
In this still, harsh embrace.

The pavement crackles underfoot,
With every step, a crunch,
Air like glass, so cold, so acute,
In silence, shadows bunch.

Clouds hang thick, a heavy veil,
Pine trees stand stark and bare,
The world feels like an ancient tale,
Trapped in winter's snare.

As night descends, time pauses,
Stars emerge, glimmering hope,
A silence wrapped in causes,
In still breaths, we softly cope.

The chill draws closer still,
Fingers numb, spirits fight,
Yet within, a hidden thrill,
To hold the dark, to embrace the light.

Silence Surrendered to Ice

Stillness blankets every shore,
In the dawn, a hushed tone,
Nature whispers, peace restored,
Cold rivulets of stone.

Branches wear a coat of dreams,
Glass-like, shimmering bright,
Echoes dance in silver streams,
Beneath the soft moonlight.

Horizon bends in shades of white,
Veils of frost, a gentle sigh,
In the heart of winter's night,
Time drifts on, slow and shy.

Every breath a note of pause,
Inhaling beauty, crystal clear,
Frozen rivers, nature's cause,
Offer solace, year by year.

From the silence, stories grow,
Icicles drip their silent tune,
In the winter's tender glow,
Frost and sorrow are in bloom.

Forgotten Voices Under Snow

In the depths of winter's hold,
A tapestry lies unfurled,
Echoes of memories, bold,
Buried deep within the world.

Footsteps frozen in the cold,
Tales that time has left behind,
Whispers of the brave and bold,
Linger softly in the mind.

The earth is draped in silence deep,
Stories hush beneath the white,
Frosted dreams that we can't keep,
Glow like stars in the night.

Voices lost in icy waltz,
Nostalgia drifts on the breeze,
Every whisper, every pulse,
Seeks to find its heart's ease.

From the layers, warmth will rise,
As spring beckons with its song,
In the snow, the heart complies,
To the love that flows along.

Veils of Icy Tranquility

Moonlit whispers softly glow,
Casting shadows on the snow.
A world wrapped in silver lace,
Time stands still in this quiet space.

Breath of winter, crisp and clear,
Echoes linger, drawing near.
Every flake, a secret told,
In the silence, silence bold.

Nature's canvas, painted white,
Stars above, a gentle light.
Veils of ice that softly sway,
Guard the dreams of yesterday.

Frosted branches, still and wise,
Underneath the veiled skies.
In this realm where time has paused,
Beauty rests, forever lost.

In this trance, we lose our way,
Yet find solace in the sway.
Veils of icy calm embrace,
Holding still the heart’s own pace.

Secrets Beneath the Ice

Beneath the ice, a world unseen,
Whispers of what might have been.
Glimmers of life, frozen tight,
Holding shadows in the night.

Ripples dance under the frost,
Echoes of the warmth we lost.
Fragile dreams in cold repose,
Nature's truth in quiet flows.

Stories buried, deep and shy,
Waiting for the spring to cry.
In the stillness, secrets lie,
Beneath the vast and watchful sky.

Frozen portraits, time's embrace,
Hide the beauty, hide the grace.
Yet, with patience, they will show,
Life's resilience, deep below.

While the winter holds it tight,
Life stirs soft beneath the white.
Secrets hidden, waiting still,
For the thaw to bend their will.

Chilled Moments in Time

Each moment caught in icy breath,
A dance of life and whispered death.
Time unfolds with gentle sighs,
In frozen frames, the spirit flies.

Frosted petals, pale and bright,
Stillness reigns in pale moonlight.
Time stands still, the world asleep,
In chilled moments, memories keep.

Glistening echoes fade away,
In the trance of winter's play.
Every silence holds a tale,
Of whispered winds and freezing hail.

Glimmering shards of past embrace,
Caught in nature's cold, sweet grace.
Time, like snow, begins to drift,
In every flake, a fleeting gift.

With every breath, we feel the chill,
Life’s soft whispers, never still.
Chilled moments weave a thread so fine,
Through the fabric of our time.

Stillness Beneath the Surface

Calm waters hide a world below,
Silence speaks what hearts may know.
Stillness reigns in twilight hue,
Depths conceal what is most true.

Beneath the surface, life abides,
Cradled where the darkness hides.
Everything waits in tranquil streams,
Shadows dance like fleeting dreams.

Ripples whisper, tales untold,
Secrets glisten, ancient gold.
In the stillness, strength takes form,
Weathering the quiet storm.

Crisp reflections, mirror bright,
Guide the heart through the night.
Stillness brings a solemn grace,
One with nature's soft embrace.

As we gaze upon the calm,
Feel the pulse, the hidden balm.
Stillness beneath the surface lies,
A sanctuary for the wise.

Dreams Entombed in Ice

Silence wraps the frozen ground,
Whispers lost, no echo found.
Frigid hopes lie deep within,
Waiting for the warmth to begin.

Shattered visions, shards of light,
Through the winter's endless night.
Ghostly figures dance in frost,
In this world, all seems lost.

Frozen rivers, dreams trapped tight,
Beneath the chill of ghostly white.
Memories glimmer, faint and pale,
A bittersweet, unyielding veil.

Yet in the cold, a flicker glows,
A promise hidden ‘neath the snow.
When spring awakens, ice will melt,
And dreams reborn will be felt.

The thaw shall bring new shapes to form,
From icy depths, a heart reborn.
Hope unfurls like blooming leaves,
From frozen dreams, the spirit weaves.

Pathways of the Hushed Mystic

In shadows deep where secrets dwell,
A silent truth begins to swell.
Footsteps trace the ancient stone,
Echoes whisper, yet alone.

Moonlight guides the wandering soul,
Through twisted paths towards the goal.
Each step unfolds a hidden tale,
Where silence weaves a tranquil veil.

Veiled in mist, the air is still,
Every breath a bending will.
Patterns swirl, unseen hands play,
On dreams that drift and sway away.

The heart beats soft within the night,
As stars above twinkle bright.
In this silence, magic brews,
As spirits dance with gentle hues.

Through the darkness, wisdom flows,
In hushed tones where the mystic grows.
Let the stillness take its part,
And guide you with its quiet heart.

Frosted Compositions of Still Air

Beneath the frost, a canvas breathes,
Nature's art, in silence weaves.
Every flake a whispered tune,
As light reflects the silver moon.

Branches bow with laden grace,
Encased in ice, their elegant lace.
Stillness reigns, no rush, no sound,
In this moment, life is crowned.

The world is hushed, yet full of dreams,
As frozen whispers trace the streams.
Colors muted, soft and light,
In this tranquil winter's night.

Frosted breaths in crisp, pure air,
Shapes arise, a beauty rare.
In stillness, we find our ease,
Wrapped in frost, a gentle freeze.

Each frozen note, a song unplayed,
In this silence, hearts are laid.
Let the coolness fill your heart,
As frozen compositions start.

Solitary Echoes Beneath Stars

Underneath the vast, dark sky,
A single voice begins to cry.
Echoes linger, drift away,
In the night, where dreams may sway.

Stars above like distant flames,
Whisper softly, calling names.
In solitude, the heart can chance,
To find its rhythm, learn to dance.

Waves of silence gently rise,
Beneath the gaze of ancient eyes.
Each twinkle, a story spun,
Of midnight journeys never done.

Lonely hearts find solace here,
In the darkness, lost yet near.
Beneath the stars, the echoes trace,
A bond that time cannot erase.

So let the night enfold your pain,
In celestial arms, break the chain.
For every echo finds its peace,
As solitary whispers cease.

Atmosphere of Cold Shadows

In the depths where whispers dwell,
Cold shadows weave a silent spell.
Moonlight dances on frost-kissed ground,
Lost echoes linger without sound.

Veils of mist embrace the night,
Stars above dim their bright light.
Every breath a fragile sigh,
As autumn leaves begin to fly.

The chilling breeze on weary bones,
Carries secrets, ancient groans.
Underneath the pines so tall,
Nature holds a frozen thrall.

Glimmers of white in darkened trees,
Whispers carried on the breeze.
In this space where shadows glide,
Life stands still, in cold divide.

Night descends, a heavy cloak,
In the silence, hearts provoke.
Beneath the vast and starry dome,
Cold shadows whisper tales of home.

Silence like Snowfall

Falling softly from the sky,
Snowflakes drift, a gentle sigh.
In the hush of winter's reign,
Voices fade like distant rain.

Blankets thick on earth's cold breast,
Nature pauses for its rest.
Every flake a silent prayer,
Whispers linger in the air.

Footsteps muffled by soft white dust,
In this magic, we all trust.
Moonlight bathes the world in peace,
As time itself begins to cease.

Branches bow with weight profound,
In this stillness, thoughts unbound.
Let the quiet softly fall,
A tranquil heart, a gentle call.

In the silence, warmth we find,
Frosty air, yet hearts aligned.
Here in snow, we lose our fear,
In every flake, a dream draws near.

A Lullaby of Glacial Hush

Underneath the icy dome,
Whispers sing of quiet home.
Crystalline dreams woven tight,
Through the fabric of the night.

Frozen rivers softly hum,
In their cadence, peace will come.
Every note a calming breath,
A lullaby that conquers death.

Sleepy clouds drift far above,
In this stillness, find our love.
Gentle hands of winter's chill,
Cradle us and time stands still.

Stars like diamonds, poised and bright,
Gift a sense of endless light.
In this slumber, shadows fade,
From our fears, we are remade.

As the night wraps all in care,
Feel the warmth, the knowing stare.
In the glacial hush we trust,
Hearts entwined, in rest we must.

Chilling Echoes of Thought

Echoes linger in the breeze,
Thoughts are frozen, hearts uneased.
Whispers piercing through the night,
As the world is bathed in white.

In the silence, doubts arise,
Beneath the cold, a mask of lies.
Frozen steps on earthy ground,
Chilling echoes, truth is found.

Beneath the weight of falling snow,
Contemplations softly flow.
In the dark, the mind does race,
Searching for a hidden place.

Thoughts like shadows in the dark,
Flicker, dance, a fleeting spark.
Each heartbeat is a whispered plea,
In the silence, set thoughts free.

Yet, in this stillness, beauty grows,
In the chill, the spirit glows.
Chilling echoes, soft and clear,
Awaken dreams that persevere.

Echoes in a Shattered World

Whispers linger through cracked stone,
Forgotten tales of dust and bone.
Silence weaves in shades of gray,
Lost voices fade, then drift away.

Shadows dance on barren ground,
Echoes of laughter, no more sound.
Time moves slow, like drifting fog,
A heart once strong, now just a bog.

Glimmers of hope in broken glass,
Memories fade, but moments pass.
Life attempts to find its song,
Yet here it feels so very wrong.

Through the ruins, dreams do roam,
A yearning deep for a lost home.
Each step echoes, a haunting wail,
In a shattered world, hopes grow frail.

Yet in despair, some sparks ignite,
A flicker in the heart so bright.
From ashes, strength begins to rise,
In shattered worlds, we seek the skies.

Winter's Breath Unheard

In the stillness of the night,
Frosty whispers take their flight.
Snowflakes dance on whispered air,
The world awaits, silent, bare.

Branches bow with heavy white,
Stars above shine cold and bright.
Winter’s breath upon my face,
Time stands still, a frozen grace.

Footprints lead to paths unknown,
Echoes fade, the night has grown.
A fire burns within my heart,
Yet from warmth, the chill won’t part.

Frozen streams and silent trees,
Whispers float upon the breeze.
Nature's hush, a sacred bond,
In winter's grasp, we still respond.

With each flake, a story spun,
In quiet moments, dreams begun.
Winter's breath, both cold and true,
Unheard melodies, waiting for you.

Still Waters of the North

Reflections deep, a tranquil time,
Ripples dance in rhythm, rhyme.
Beneath the pines, the waters gleam,
A hidden world, a waking dream.

Misty mornings greet the dawn,
Nature's canvas softly drawn.
In silence lies a language pure,
The stillness speaks, hearts reassured.

Gentle whispers in the breeze,
Carrying secrets through the trees.
Echoing thoughts of what was lost,
In still waters, we find the cost.

Life unravels, threads unwind,
Yet peace is what we hope to find.
Moments captured, forever still,
In nature's heart, we forge our will.

So let the waters guide our way,
Through winding paths, both night and day.
In stillness, solace feels so near,
The North whispers, our souls to steer.

Frosted Dreams Unraveled

Frosted whispers on the breeze,
Dreams that linger, hopes that seize.
Nature's breath, a chilling sigh,
Beneath the gray and solemn sky.

In twilight's grasp, shadows creep,
Silent promises, secrets keep.
A world of white, so soft and deep,
Yet deep within, the heart must weep.

Each snowflake falls, a fleeting chance,
To live anew, to start a dance.
But as they land, they drift away,
In bitter cold, they cannot stay.

Time unravels like threads undone,
In frosted dreams, we search for sun.
Echoes of laughter, warmth of souls,
A quest for peace that forever rolls.

Yet through the frost, we brave the chill,
In moments lost, we find our will.
Frosted dreams may fade from view,
But in our hearts, they still hold true.

Whispers in the Snow

Softly fall the crystals,
Glistening like tiny stars,
Each one tells a secret,
Boundless whispers from afar.

Trees wearing crowns of white,
Silent tales of winter's breath,
Nature's quilt, pure and bright,
Embracing life in gentle death.

Footsteps muffled, quieted,
In the stillness, hearts will roam,
Finding solace in the chill,
Finding warmth in winter's home.

A world wrapped in silence,
Underneath a frosted dome,
Where dreams of spring grow bold,
Beneath this cold, tranquil tome.

Listen close, the snow will speak,
In the hush, a soft embrace,
Whispers linger, rich and deep,
In this frozen, sacred space.

Shards of Quietude

Beneath the icy canopy,
Stillness weaves its gentle art,
Silent shards around me lay,
As the world slows, heart by heart.

In the crystal-laden air,
Dreams emerge, elusive, slight,
Fragments caught in whispered prayer,
Lost to day, but found in night.

Shadows curl in muted light,
Time dissolves within the breeze,
Moments drift like feathered flight,
Nestled in the patient trees.

Each breath slows, the mind unwinds,
Pondering what silence brings,
In this calm, a peace unwinds,
Like the echo of soft wings.

Embrace the shards of quietude,
Let them dance in your serene,
In this realm of solitude,
Find the tranquil in the keen.

Echoes of a Still Winter

Frost kisses the barren ground,
Echoes linger, soft and low,
Winter’s breath, a haunting sound,
Tales of yore in flurries flow.

Shadowed branches bare and stark,
Ghostly whispers through the trees,
In the chill, there lies a spark,
A warmth hidden, like a tease.

Footfalls trace a soft refrain,
Where the silence hums and sighs,
In the quiet, peace remains,
Underneath the leaden skies.

Time suspended, moments freeze,
In the grip of winter's reign,
Echoes carried on the breeze,
Melodies of a soft chain.

Listen well to winter’s song,
In the quiet, find your grace,
Each note flows, both sweet and strong,
In the silence, a warm embrace.

Frosted Dreams in Hibernation

Nestled deep in winter's hold,
Dreams lie resting, safe and warm,
Frosted visions, silent, bold,
Awaiting spring's embracing charm.

Underneath the layers thick,
Life pulses, waiting for the thaw,
Whispers soft as heartbeats quick,
In a world that seems to draw.

Nights stretch long and days grow short,
Starlit skies cradle the night,
Each moment holds a soft report,
Of dreams tucked in, out of sight.

With each frost, a tale is spun,
Nature sleeps but never fades,
In the quiet, warmth is won,
In the dark, the light cascades.

Awake, arrive the sunny days,
When dreams take flight and body stirs,
From hibernation’s tender gaze,
All the world in blooms concurs.

A Symphony of Stillness

In the hush of dawn's embrace,
Whispers weave through empty space.
Nature holds its breath so tight,
The world prepares for gentle light.

Trees stand tall, a silent choir,
Each leaf a note, a soft desire.
The breeze becomes a tender song,
As peace prevails, where hearts belong.

Clouds drift slowly, painted grey,
Carrying dreams of yesterday.
The brook gurgles, a quiet tune,
Beneath the watchful, silver moon.

Time appears to pause and wait,
In this realm, we contemplate.
Moments stretch like webs of silk,
In the calm, we find our milk.

As day breaks with its golden glow,
The symphony begins to flow.
Each sound, a brush against the ear,
In stillness, we dissolve our fear.

Thorns of Frost in the Afternoon

Winter's breath paints all in white,
Crystal thorns shimmer in the light.
Nature sleeps beneath the veil,
A frozen world, quiet and pale.

Trees wear coats of icy lace,
Every branch a delicate trace.
Sunlight dances on the frost,
Beauty found, though warmth is lost.

Footsteps crunch on powdered ground,
Echoes linger, sharp and round.
A chilling breeze whispers low,
Secrets only winter knows.

In this realm of stark contrast,
The moment's stillness holds us fast.
Time feels slow and almost sweet,
As nature's symphony, we meet.

Thorns of frost, so sharp, precise,
Glimmers of a cold paradise.
In the quiet after the storm,
The world lies still, yet feels so warm.

Moonlit Shadows on Snow

Beneath the moon's soft silver gaze,
Snowflakes twinkle in a daze.
Shadows play on fields so wide,
Whispers of the night abide.

Footprints trace the paths of dreams,
Silent echoes, soft moonbeams.
The world transforms in softest white,
As stars twinkle with delight.

Cool air wraps around like silk,
A soothing balm, as rich as milk.
Night's embrace feels calm and pure,
In stillness, hearts begin to stir.

Trees cast shapes that sway and bend,
In the shadows, time can suspend.
Each breath a cloud that fades away,
In moonlit whispers, we shall stay.

As night unfolds its velvet cloak,
And silence sings, no words are spoke.
In the depths of winter's glow,
Peace resides in the falling snow.

Crystalline Echoes of Solitude

In a realm where silence reigns,
Crystalline echoes dance like chains.
Thoughts drift softly through the air,
In solitude, we learn to care.

Each breath a whisper of the heart,
A sacred space, a work of art.
Loneliness, a friend so dear,
In its arms, we shed our fear.

Winter's chill wraps us in lace,
Moments freeze, we slow our pace.
In the quiet, we begin to find,
The gentle rhythm of the mind.

Reflections bounce on frosted panes,
Carrying the weight of dreams and pains.
Through stillness, wisdom starts to bloom,
In solitude, we dispel the gloom.

Crystalline echoes call us near,
In their song, we shed our tear.
A journey deep within our soul,
In silence, we become whole.

Muffled Echoes of Solitude

In shadows deep, whispers roam,
Secrets linger, far from home.
A heart beats soft, alone it sighs,
In the stillness, silence lies.

Echoes bounce from empty walls,
Where once were laughter, now just calls.
Ghosts of memories dance and fade,
In the quiet, hope is swayed.

Time drips slowly, like the rain,
Each droplet carries hidden pain.
Notes of sorrow fill the air,
Yet solace blooms, if one would dare.

Outside the world, a distant roar,
But inside here, I search for more.
In tangled thoughts, I often weave,
The fabric of what I believe.

Yet still, in darkness, light can gleam,
A flicker weak, but still a dream.
Amidst the echoes, a soft plea,
To find the self that longs to be.

Stillness Cradling the Night

The moonlit sky, a velvet shroud,
Whispers hush, hush the crowd.
Stars like candles softly gleam,
In the stillness, dreams redeem.

Cool breezes weave through branches bare,
Wrapping silence, tender care.
Night unfolds like a secret tome,
In the dark, I feel at home.

Distant shadows start to play,
Echoes of the fading day.
Each moment holds a breath so light,
Cradled gently by the night.

Crickets chirp their lullabies,
As time dissolves beneath the skies.
Nature breathes, a soft refrain,
In quietude, we find our gain.

With each heartbeat, the world slows down,
In this peace, no need for crown.
Just the stars, the moon, and me,
In stillness, I am finally free.

Unseen Flakes in the Void

In the void where silence dwells,
Drift the whispers, no one tells.
Unseen flakes of time and space,
Hold the echoes of a face.

Invisible threads of fate align,
Twirling softly, fragile vine.
In the air, they gently weave,
A tapestry of what to believe.

Beyond the gaze of human eyes,
Lies a beauty, a soft surprise.
Particles dance in ethereal light,
In the void, shadows ignite.

Each fragment holds a story's breath,
Fleeting glimpses of life and death.
In the stillness, truth is set,
In the unknown, we are met.

Yet even in this emptiness found,
Magic stirs without a sound.
Unseen flakes, so thin, so bold,
In the void, the secrets unfold.

Emptiness Draped in White

A canvas bare, is stark and bright,
Emptiness draped in tranquil white.
Snowflakes fall like whispered dreams,
In the quiet, hope redeems.

Blanket of peace, the world inhales,
Footprints lost in untouched trails.
In this silence, echoes fade,
As the heart becomes unmade.

Each flake's descent tells a tale,
Of journeys large, both grand and pale.
In the still, we find release,
Wrapped in softness, we find peace.

The chill bites but feels so near,
In solitude, there's nothing to fear.
Beneath the white, we start to grow,
As the world whispers soft and low.

Emptiness found in nature's glow,
A sanctuary where we go.
In every stark and quiet sight,
Lies the promise of pure light.

Ghosts of Frosted Pines

In the stillness, whispers sigh,
Beneath the boughs where shadows lie.
Frosty tendrils touch the ground,
Nature's silence, lost, profound.

Figures dance in brittle light,
Eerie tales of winter's night.
Among the branches, secrets blend,
Echoes of the seasons' end.

Each breath frozen in the air,
Memories wrapped in cold despair.
The moon watches with a gaze,
As the world drifts in a haze.

A canvas white, untouched, pure,
Time flows slowly, yet unsure.
Ghostly forms in frozen grace,
Nature's spirit, still to chase.

So let the night enfold the trees,
In gentle sighs upon the breeze.
For in these pines, the stories weave,
A tale of frost, of those who leave.

The Hushed Heart of Winter

Snowflakes whisper soft and low,
Blanketing the world in glow.
In each flake, a secret lies,
Beneath the gray, the silence cries.

Frosted kisses on the ground,
In every corner, dreams are found.
Trees stand tall, their branches bare,
Holding the weight of winter's stare.

The air is crisp, a tender bite,
Stars flicker in the velvet night.
Embers glow from hearths nearby,
Warmth wraps close, as shadows fly.

Time moves slow in frosted light,
Days turn into endless night.
But in this hush, a heartbeat waits,
Winter's soul, that contemplates.

While snowflakes fall, the world stands still,
The heart of winter—deep and chill.
Listen close, let memories stir,
In the quiet, find the blur.

Icy Reflections in Twilight

The sun dips low, casting its glow,
A painted sky, a canvas slow.
Ice crystals shimmer on the lake,
Mirrored dreams that twilight makes.

With each ripple, memories dance,
Captured moments in a trance.
Beneath the surface, stories breathe,
Of summer's warmth, now a wreath.

Branches dangle, draped in white,
Nature's lace against the night.
In the stillness, echoes call,
Icy reflections, holding all.

As dusk descends, the stars take flight,
Guiding hopes through the fleeting night.
Shadows stretch, the world restores,
As dreams weave through open doors.

So watch the lake as daylight fades,
In icy depths, where peace cascades.
For what is lost, we'll hold it tight,
In the twilight's soft, glowing light.

Serenity Beneath the Snow

Quiet blankets the sleeping ground,
Whispers of peace in silence found.
The world transforms, all muffled sound,
In the hush, sweet dreams abound.

Gentle flakes in sweet ballet,
Filling paths where children play.
Each step soft, a tender grace,
Winter's whisper, warm embrace.

Branches bow with heavy weight,
Nature's beauty, calm, sedate.
In the stillness, hearts align,
Finding solace, pure, divine.

As shadows lengthen, stars arise,
The moon glimmers, silvered skies.
A world transformed in softest light,
Guided by the stars at night.

So let the snow fall soft and low,
And wrap the earth in peace to grow.
In serenity, we find release,
A winter's night, a heart at peace.

Embrace of a Frozen Moment

In winter's hush, the world stands still,
A breath of time, against our will.
The frost, it dances on the air,
Embracing dreams without a care.

Snowflakes twirl in soft embrace,
Each one unique, a fleeting grace.
Moments frozen, hearts beat slow,
In silence, whispers start to grow.

The sunlight glimmers on the white,
A canvas pure, a world of light.
Each crystal shines, a story told,
Captured dreams in the bitter cold.

As shadows stretch and daylight fades,
We hold on tight, as time cascades.
In silence deep, we find our peace,
In frozen frames, all worries cease.

Let's linger here, in love's soft glow,
Where every moment starts to flow.
In stillness, we have come to see,
The beauty found in you and me.

Whispers Beneath the Ice

Beneath the surface, secrets lie,
Echoes of dreams that never die.
Whispers softly call the night,
Silent songs of pure delight.

The world above, so cold and gray,
Bears witness to the tales we say.
In hidden depths, our hearts will beat,
As frozen rivers, softly meet.

Crackling stillness fills the air,
A pause of breath, a moment rare.
While shadows dance in frigid light,
With tales of warmth that feel so right.

What lives beneath, we cannot see,
Yet feels the same as you and me.
An ice-bound world, yet life persists,
In every touch, in every mist.

So listen closely, hear the tone,
Of nature's heart, forever known.
Beneath the ice, where dreams can sleep,
Whispers of love in silence deep.

Crystal Veils of Stillness

A world wrapped tight in crystal veils,
As winter whispers, softly trails.
The earth adorned in frosty lace,
Each flake a gem, a fleeting grace.

In stillness caught, we find our thread,
Where frozen paths of silence spread.
A gentle hush, a quiet sigh,
As moments linger, time drifts by.

Snowy branches sway so slow,
Carrying whispers where dreams flow.
In glistening light, the shadows play,
Creating art in nature's way.

The sun dips low, a golden hue,
Painting the ice in shades anew.
In twilight's glow, we feel the peace,
As nature offers sweet release.

Within these veils, our spirits soar,
In frozen stillness, we want more.
A tender touch in winter's breath,
Embraced by life, beyond the death.

So let us roam in this serene,
Where crystal dreams become our scene.
In stillness, love, we find our home,
In icy realms, forever roam.

Laughter of Falling Snowflakes

Snowflakes tumble, dance and glide,
Whispers of laughter in their stride.
Softly landing, a fleeting play,
Brightening hearts on a winter's day.

Each flake a story, unique and new,
Painting the world in a coat of blue.
Children's laughter fills the air,
Joy ignited, without a care.

Twinkling lights on icy trees,
A winter wonder, hearts at ease.
Nature's touch, pure and light,
Moments cherished, pure delight.

Snowball fights, a friendly race,
Time stands still in this sacred space.
With each swirl, the world seems bright,
In falling snow, we find our light.

So let us gather, hold on tight,
In winter's arms, everything’s right.
For laughter echoes, warm and true,
In laughter of snowflakes, me and you.

Silhouettes in Winter Light

Amidst the branches, shadows play,
Silhouettes dance at end of day.
A golden hue, a soft embrace,
Nature's canvas, a timeless grace.

Frosted windows, whispers clear,
Winter's magic, drawing near.
Figures twirl in twilight's glow,
A silent waltz, in ebb and flow.

Soft footsteps crunch on frozen ground,
In this stillness, peace is found.
Light filters through the trees so tall,
Creating art, enchanting all.

Each shadow tells a tale of night,
Of fleeting dreams in soft twilight.
Hues of amber, lavender skies,
In winter’s grasp, time gently flies.

As stars awaken, shadows blend,
In winter light, all sorrows mend.
A serene moment, pure and bright,
In silhouettes, we find our flight.

The Glistening Solitude

In the quiet hush of winter's call,
A glistening solitude blankets all.
Each frozen breath hangs in the air,
A tranquil whisper, pure and rare.

Icicles sparkle, gems of ice,
In this stillness, we pay the price.
The world is hushed, wrapped in white,
A secret kept, away from sight.

Footprints trace in soft, deep snow,
Paths of longing, where dreams flow.
Underneath the crescent moon,
Loneliness sings a quiet tune.

If one listens, silence speaks,
In solitude, the heart seeks.
Moments frozen, yet they flow,
In glistening solitude, we grow.

So close your eyes, embrace this space,
Let the stillness, your thoughts race.
Find yourself in winter's peace,
A glistening solitude, sweet release.

Landscapes of Muffled Sound

The world outside is hushed and still,
A winter landscape, calm and chill.
Snow blankets all in soft repose,
Where whispers linger, and silence grows.

Trees stand tall in coats of white,
Guardians of this peaceful night.
The air is crisp, a sharp delight,
As shadows stretch in fading light.

Footsteps echo on snow’s white crust,
Each crunch a promise, each sound a trust.
In nooks and crannies, secrets hide,
In landscapes vast, where dreams reside.

The wind carries tales of yore,
A gentle sigh, a distant lore.
In the stillness, we hear the call,
Of nature’s heartbeat, connecting all.

So wander forth in winter's trance,
And let the quiet invite you to dance.
In landscapes of muffled sound,
Find beauty in stillness, all around.

Until the Sun Awakens

In the stillness of dawn's embrace,
Shadows dance in a warm, soft glow.
Whispers linger, secrets trace,
Night's gentle grip starts to let go.

Colors bloom as dreams take flight,
Silence fades into morning's hue.
Hope awakens, a new delight,
As the world begins anew.

Birds sing sweet in joyful refrain,
Daylight spills over the land.
Sunrise breaks the night's last chain,
A golden touch, the day's command.

With every ray, life starts to stir,
Nature wakes from slumber deep.
An orchestra of sound, a gentle purr,
In the heart of spring, dreams leap.

Until the sun, bright and bold,
Paints the sky with tales to tell.
In its warmth, our stories unfold,
A promise held in light’s soft shell.

An Arctic Lullaby

Under the blanket of shimmering white,
A world of silence, vast and deep.
Stars twinkle softly in the night,
As the universe sighs in sleep.

Whispers of frost cling to the air,
While the moon bathes all in its glow.
Lone winds carry tales beyond compare,
Where icy rivers quietly flow.

In the distance, a seabird calls,
Echoes of solitude in the chill.
Glacial giants stand, time enthralls,
Guardians of secrets, silent and still.

Snowflakes dance as dreams take flight,
Each one a promise in the dark.
In this realm of wonder and fright,
Nature's poetry leaves its mark.

Wrapped in the arms of winter's song,
Embrace the cold, let worries pass.
Within this beauty, we all belong,
In the heart of the frozen expanse.

Tomorrow in Ice and Silence

Tomorrow holds a world of white,
Carved from dreams and frozen sighs.
In the stillness, the stars ignite,
A canvas stretched across the skies.

Each flake a promise, softly spun,
Drifting down, a delicate breath.
Under the watchful Arctic sun,
We find beauty in whispered death.

Frosted branches, a glistening sight,
With rime that sings of winter's tale.
The night holds secrets, pure and bright,
While shadows weave through a silver veil.

Hope awaits in the morning light,
As silence echoes through the pine.
In this realm where peace takes flight,
We discover hearts that intertwine.

Tomorrow comes on icy beams,
With a hush that calms the mind.
In the stillness, we share our dreams,
And leave the noise of life behind.

Threads of Snow and Solitude

In a world woven from threads of snow,
The quiet whispers secrets untold.
Footprints fade where cold winds blow,
As the heart embraces the bold.

Silence dances on frozen streams,
While time drapes its fabric, soft and pure.
In solitude, we find our dreams,
Wrapped in stillness, our thoughts demure.

Each flake that falls is a story spun,
Tracing paths where few have fared.
Under the gaze of the winter sun,
We seek solace, unafraid and shared.

Candles flicker in the twilight chill,
Casting shadows on the walls of time.
In this cozy nook, our spirits fill,
With warmth found in the simplest rhyme.

Threads of snow connect the night,
Binding us to this quiet place.
In solitude, our hearts take flight,
Finding joy in winter's embrace.

Resonance of the Chilling Void

In the stillness of the night,
A hollow echo calls my name,
Stars blink softly in their flight,
Embraced by this endless flame.

The shadows stretch across the way,
Whispers linger in the dark,
Lost among the dreams that sway,
A silence sings, igniting spark.

Frosted breath dances in the air,
A solitude that chills the bone,
Here I stand, alone, and bare,
In the void, my thoughts are sown.

Time drips slowly on the ground,
Moments frozen, etched in ice,
In this cavern, truth is found,
Resonating, casting dice.

Yet within this chilling sweep,
A faint glimmer starts to rise,
From the depths, dreams softly creep,
Illuminating darkened skies.

Glistening Oceans of Silence

Beneath the waves of silver light,
Where thoughts drift like a ship's sail,
A vast expanse, serene and bright,
Whispers of the deep prevail.

In the depths, a stillness lingers,
The heartbeat of the ocean's soul,
Each wave sings with gentle fingers,
Caressing shores, a timeless roll.

Stars above, reflections dance,
Mirrored in the ocean's face,
Here I find a fleeting chance,
To lose myself in endless space.

The horizon beckons, calm and wide,
A call that fills the void within,
Sailing forth, on silent tide,
In a world where dreams begin.

Glistening waves of peace surround,
In this ocean's tender sway,
Echoing a soothing sound,
As silence holds the night at bay.

Whispering Winds Through Frozen Trees

Amidst the branches, cold and bare,
The whispers swirl like autumn's song,
Each gust a tale, a breath to share,
Through frosted boughs where shadows throng.

The landscape draped in silver hue,
A tranquil scene, a winter's veil,
Beneath the sky, a quiet blue,
In harmony, the winds set sail.

Echoes of past dreams take flight,
Carried softly on the breeze,
Through the night that holds the light,
A rhythm found among the trees.

They sway and bend in chill embrace,
Guardians of secrets, whispered low,
In frozen stillness, a sacred space,
Where nature's heart continues to flow.

Underneath their icy shroud,
Hope awaits, a warming glow,
In every gust, a voice is loud,
Whispering stories of the snow.

Cold Embrace of Loneliness

In the stillness, shadows creep,
A heavy heart, a mind so slow,
Wrapped in layers, tight and deep,
Loneliness begins to grow.

Silent echoes fill the space,
A ghost of laughter haunts my mind,
In the mirror, a vacant face,
Searching for what's left behind.

Frosted windows filter light,
A chill that seeps beneath the skin,
Each moment stretches into night,
A battle lost, where to begin?

Yet in this cold, I find a plea,
A whisper soft, a thread of hope,
In solitude, I start to see,
The fragile ways in which we cope.

An embrace that feels like stone,
Yet within, a fire starts to rise,
In loneliness, I'm never alone,
For in the silence, courage lies.

Silence Wrapped in Snowflakes

Softly falling from the grey,
Each snowflake dances, finds its way.
Whispers hush the world around,
In this stillness, peace is found.

Bare branches cradle frozen sighs,
Underneath the muted skies.
Footsteps muffled, hearts at ease,
Wrapped in warmth, a gentle breeze.

Nature's blanket, pure and white,
The quiet glows in fading light.
Moments linger, time stands still,
In the hush, we find our will.

Frosted dreams in twilight's embrace,
Every flake a unique trace.
The air feels crisp, the world aglow,
In silence wrapped, we softly flow.

A canvas bright, with shadows play,
Stillness reigns as night holds sway.
Snowflakes whisper, melt away,
Leaving silence, come what may.

Timeless Whisper of the Ice

Beneath the glassy surface bright,
Echoes of the past take flight.
Frozen whispers tell their tale,
Silent secrets in the pale.

Ripples linger, memories chase,
In the stillness, find their place.
Nature's breath, a gentle sigh,
Here in stillness, time slips by.

Glistening shapes in winter's light,
Every sparkle, pure delight.
Timeless stories softly spun,
In the quiet, all is one.

An ancient dance of frost and air,
Life’s reflections floating there.
In each moment, peace bestowed,
As the ice reveals the road.

Crystals shimmer, shadows dart,
A fleeting world, yet close to heart.
In the chill, a warmth resides,
Timeless whispers, nature guides.

Unbreakable Calm of the Frosted Earth

Each breath carries a frozen tune,
Fields lie still beneath the moon.
In the grip of winter's hold,
Secrets of the earth unfold.

Silvery mists softly glide,
Nature's calm, a hidden guide.
Echoes keen, the silence reigns,
In this stillness, peace remains.

Frosted paths and crystal trees,
Whispers carried on the breeze.
Moments wrapped in icy grace,
Finding solace, we embrace.

Covers deep, the earth asleep,
In the quiet, thoughts we keep.
Frosted treasures, serene and bright,
Unbreakable calm in the night.

Each frozen flake, a dream to hold,
Stories shared as night grows cold.
In this tranquil, silent zone,
Frosted earth, we rest, we roam.

Layers of Stillness

Beneath the weight of winter's touch,
Layers blanketing, oh so much.
Silent whispers, soft and clear,
In this stillness, we draw near.

Heartbeats hush in the frosty air,
Nature pauses, moments rare.
Every layer holds a song,
In this stillness, we belong.

With every drift, the world transforms,
A quiet scene in countless forms.
Here in layers, dreams appear,
Wrapped in stillness, calm and dear.

Footprints fade in the morning light,
Leaving traces of our flight.
Each layer thickens, yet reveals,
Unearthed truths that winter heals.

Awakened thoughts, like snowflakes fall,
In layers, wisdom calls us all.
Stillness holds the power here,
In the quiet, we draw near.

www.ingramcontent.com/pod-product-compliance
Ingram Content Group UK Ltd.
Pitfield, Milton Keynes, MK11 3LW, UK
UKHW031943151224
452382UK00006B/163

9 789916 793695